AN ANCIENT TRAGEDY

BASED ON THE GREAT INDIAN EPIC MAHABHARATA

SIDDH SHANKAR MISHRA

ISBN 979-888503655-9

I thank and pour the poetry's flower

With love and affection and honor's shower-

To the teachers of mine I always incline

They taught me so high, they taught me so fine

How repay for their, those hard and fair

Being a poet despite, a word is rare

The friends, colleagues and comrades on my part

I thank to them from deepest of my heart

Cooperation I got encouragement I found

Can you compare it for coin and pound?

No credit to me but goes to them all

Though I created this collection small

Contents

Foreword

Dear readers! I am not a very big poet or writer as the great literary individuals are. I am just a simple and general teacher. English is not natural to me as I have passed each part of my life in my village living among Hindi speaking people. English is a language learned by me with a very hard work and practice still having errors. I could never acquire a high class study of English. I started studying it from class 6 in government Junior high school in my village. My journey of learning formal education of English was ended when I passed intermediate as I got admitted for B.Sc with Hindi medium. But I kept on my self-study of poetic sense and English grammar as much as I could do as an English teacher. In earlier days I started writing Hindi poems and articles as it was my natural tongue. But in later days when I thought that I had acquired sufficient understanding of English I started writing in English too. The beginning was there with some small poems. I still remember my first poem of four lines-

This is a small family our institute
Good are teachers very-very them I salute
All the students, friends of us they are very cute
This is heaven-like place here is all the bute

It impressed some of my fellows as well as me also, and I got a satisfactory beginning. Even today I don't have as much knowledge of English as it should have been for writing a book. But it's grace of God **Lord Shiva**giving intellect to an ignorant person like me. Living in village and in lack of proper resources I couldn't acquire very good knowledge whereas I had a great interest in literature and grammar. I could not get a person who could converse with me on a topic or help me to improve my knowledge and poetic sense. I was alone and under these circumstances I have improved myself as much as I could do. So I hope that kind readers will not mind errors if any made by me. It is actually nothing less than grace of goddess mother Saraswati on me that I have dared write something not in my natural tongue. I expect that with kind affection of dear readers I will surely be successful in my task of writing this book.

Sitting lonely a day abruptly an idea stuck my mind that I should write something smart. But what and how it was still a question. Writing is a skill and to be at home in this art is not an easy task. Ideas were several in the mind but how to descend those ideas on blank pages was indeed a hard deed for a man like me. It was not less than looking for water in desert for an ordinary teacher to write like poets and writers and to copy his ideas on blank pages keeping in mind the satisfaction and curiosity of readers. Gathering courage I raised pen and began to make its relation with blank papers. **Mother Goddess Saraswati** poured her grace and with little knowledge and broken word bank this mini-book was created by this man of limited knowledge.

So it is my courteous request to all dear readers that not paying strong attention to the errors made by me make the aim of publication of the book successful.

-SIDDH SHANKAR MISHRA

PRAY TO MOTHER SARASWATI

O mother! We ever meditate-

Thy names asking for thy kind grace

Let our intellect be indulge in-

Superior deeds for humane sake

Let us see the good way O mother!

Of life whenever we go mislead

Let us be known of a certain point

Blossomed with glory delight and peace

Let us become a light of lamp

In the dark world and wide of peace

Consuming ourselves as candle's ray

But lighten the world for no claim

Let us getting the new directions

Of duty's sense forever-forever

The determination of conduct

Will truly characterize

Oh! Ocean of grace goddess mother-

Saraswati with veena's strings

Give me the knowledge of firmly stand

On pathway of duty but never move.

DEDICATED TO TEACHERS

The garden of life was drenched with ideals

Not a single plant but all, to him, are specials

Who wakes himself up at break of the day

And starts working hard in his duly scheduled way

If any plant has broken its stem

Or some new blossoms are coming to them

If any plant is leaving sprout

Seeing them with pods he feels so proud

He feels at once the woes of his beloved-

Plants. If faded any, he pours his love.

If someday someone is going to be misguide

He shows him the real and true way of life

He works harder in the day in the night

Forgets everything even the thirst or bite

He becomes happy when they are delighted

Becomes he too sad when they are frighted

He planted a garden the huge and larger

He eats its fruits? O NEVER! O NEVER!

Some men think him mere a toiler in the strife

He is not just a gardener but the producer of life

DEDICATED TO PARENTS

She gave me life he gave me life

None but my adorable parents

Thousands times adore in lotus like steps

Singing your dignity's songs forever

Ever getting the incredible blessing-

of yours. Now a little boy

Is worthy to sing is worthy to do-

A lovely chaplet clearly made of-

The pearls of words some old some new

And loitering with this for general mass

Always got affectionate love

And bless from your sacred hands

And will to get it all futurity

And will to sing for your sake

And will to intertwine the love infinite

In pearls of words but unable to search.

ABOUT THE BOOK

The book "AN ANCIENT TRAGEDY" is English version of Hindi Kavya "DYUT KARMA PHALA" written by me in 2012 published on KDP AMAZON.IN. The phrase " DYUT KARMA PHALA " means – result of gambling. It is a message to society that gambling is an ill-practice as well as it is a bad addiction of man if he indulges in gambling deeds. AN ANCIENT TRAGEDY is a poetry essence taken from one of the greatest Hindu Epic " MAHABHARATA " written by the great poetic genius "BHAGWAN VEDAVYASA". In the story, the Pandavas (the five sons of king Pandu- the king of state Hastinapur. after death of Pandu his blind brother Dhritrashtra was made king) were invited by Kauravas (hundred sons of Dhritrashtra) for playing the game of gamble. Kauravas and Pandavas were at daggers dawn. Pandavas didn't know that they were being trapped by Kauravas inviting them for gambling. So they started playing it as a normal game. But Kauravas defeated them by using deception. Pandavas lost everything they had. All the wealth, their treasury, their palace, their army, their subject, their honor, everything was lost by the Pandavas even themselves. They had to take their clothes off even in the assembly hall among all the royal authorities. Moreover they had to put their wife Draupadi (wife of all five Pandavas) on stake in hope of return their wealth and honor. But in the last stake they lost her too. Draupadi did know nothing about the incident happening in the assembly hall. When she was called there by the winning prince Duryodhana, she was too surprised to know that she had been put on stake by her husband. But she was not agreeing to come over there as she was the royal bride of the state. Then Duryodhana ordered his brother Dushashana to take Draupadi in the court forcefully. Dushashana drew Draupadi in the court dragging her on the earth seizing her hair in his hands. Seeing this disdainful scene all the courtiers in the hall were too much blushed but no one could speak a word. Draupadi tried to make a complaint against this hateful and shameful activity. But when she saw the bowed heads of all personnel she understood that there was no one who could speak a word against that injustice. In the mean time Duryodhana ordered Dushashana to draw all the clothes from Draupadi's body and make her completely naked. The crush of morality was indeed unbearable for everyone there. But no one could dare to go against the decision of Duryodhana. Even the king as well as the great warriors like Guru Dronacharya, Bhishma, Kripacharya etc. could do nothing according to law. Draupadi found herself alone however she had five husbands, father in law - king Dhritrashtra and other grand relatives. When she found herself completely, helpless she made her voice to lord Krishna and prayed to save her honor. Lord Krishna heard her summons and appeared there invisibly. As Dushashana started drawing Draupadi's sari (a strip of cloth worn by women in India) Lord Krishna did the unbelievable miracle. The sari's length kept increasing infinitely. He kept on trying to strip Draupadi for hours but couldn't do that. In the last he was so exhausted that he fell on the floor.

After it was done Draupadi could assure herself that she was safe from the hands of that cruel wild wolf. As she awakened from her pray she started saying some angry words to all the men present in that hall of stake. As she was going to make a terrible curse to entire Hastinapur state, Duryodhana's mother, the queen of the state Rani Gandhari abruptly appeared there and stopped Draupadi to do this. She suggested her not to give a curse to the whole mass as it was the power collected by her with lifetime selfless service to her husbands. Gandhari also tried to embarrass the royal men sitting in the court. She said that they look everything in life as hunting animals and playing stake. The king was so scared of Draupadi that he said to Draupadi to ask him for anything she liked. She got all her wealth and state back lost by her husband in the stake. As they were about to go from there blatant Duryodhana and his maternal uncle Shakuni formed a new strategy and made the Pandavas agree to play again with the condition that if they won they would get everything, they had lost. But if they lost they would go for 12 years banishment and 1 year hidden banishment. Pandavas lost again and they had to go for 13 years banishment.

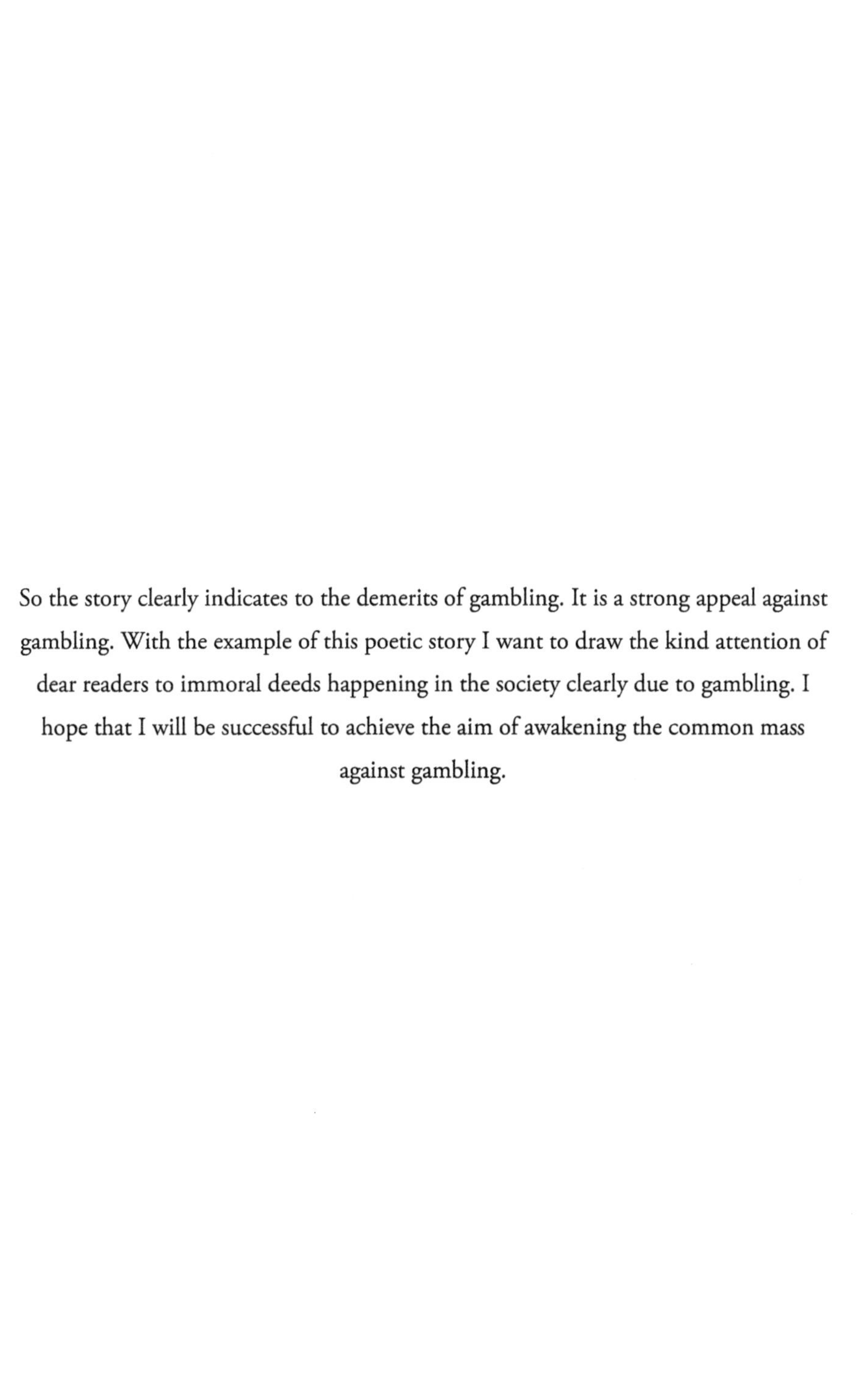

So the story clearly indicates to the demerits of gambling. It is a strong appeal against gambling. With the example of this poetic story I want to draw the kind attention of dear readers to immoral deeds happening in the society clearly due to gambling. I hope that I will be successful to achieve the aim of awakening the common mass against gambling.

1. MAJOR OBJECTS OF WRITING THIS POETRY

When I started writing this poetry essence, I thought that there must be some essential social reasons to accomplish this work. There must be some objects that can benifite the modern society and the new age. So before starting the main content I would like to draw the kind attention of the readers to some major objects revealed in this chapter.

- *GAMBLING - A MALPRACTICE TO THE SOCIETY.*
- *IMPORTANCE OF MOTHER TONGUE.*
- *LITERARY AND MYTHOLOGICAL KNOWLEDGE.*

GAMBLING - A MALPRACTICE TO THE SOCIETY

Stake, the play of dices which easily makes a common man's life uncommon. So much uncommon that he has no sign of commonness. He is neither worthy to sit among common people, nor to join the common assemblies. Everything in his life happens uncommon.

History is the witness of the fact that one could neither be great nor wealthy by gambling nor, he could get any treasure. If he has got something, that is contempt, internal perplexity, and family distress. Commonly people think stake as a quick way of earning more money. But it is possible that they do not know that the game of two for one, four for two in the last ends on zero. There are many examples in the history that having been trapped by stake and bet kings had lost their kingdoms and even their life. In ancient time when there were so limited sources of playing stake even then kings took no more time to spoil themselves. And now days, there are several resources of playing stake as well as gambling is on peak of its extension how a common man will bear with its fatal hit, this fact is considerable.

In Indian society gambling is too prevalent on the occasion of some festivals. It's a saying in India that playing stake on festivals is auspicious as well as beneficial. With the result of that people spoil their delight of festivals as well as they are compelled to tolerate the economical lack for many days. But here the question arises if the prevalence of playing stake on festivals can be accepted as a fact. Is this fact revealed in scriptures or is it certified by learned individuals and myths? Possibly not. We should trust only on those things which are revealed in scriptures and clinging with mythological certifications. Any religion or scripture has not appreciated gambling but narrating its demerits they have named it as social misconduct.

Through a mythological story the poetry ''AN ANCIENT TRAGEDY'' stimulates the common mass for uprooting the gambling activities, throwing light on the result of playing stake and expanding the message- ''gambling is a social misconduct'' expects for the success of its major object- uprooting of gambling.

THE IMPORTANCE OF MOTHER TONGUE

Narrating the need and importance of the native language the quick running and strong thought explosive writing implement of the legendary poetic genius Bhartendu Harishchandra has inaugurated the following couplet-

Nija bhasha unnati ahai, saba unnati ko mool

Binu nija bhasha gyan ke, mitey na hiya ko sool

Means one's own native language is one's progress indeed. It is the basis of all improvement and growth. Without having the knowledge of one's own mother language one can never be happy.

The thought is quite correct. The basis of all kind of evolution of man is only his mother tongue. Mother language is the language holding which finger an innocent child leads his tiny feet slowly on the path of knowledge and in later days he becomes a linguistic and prudent of Vedas.

It is a considerable fact that the officers, sitting on the highest positions and discreet, addressing the large assemblies, must have learned toddling on the path of knowledge seizing the kind finger of their mother language in their earlier academic session. It is more prevalent in India that in the expanding field of knowledge and in the dignity of getting higher official and social positions people feel embarrassment in pronouncing words of their own mother tongue. And they feel very proud when they pronounce the words of any foreign language- it's too embarrassing.

The modern man in India particularly youth, in spite of having insufficient knowledge of English, think status symbol (sign of high class life style) using English words in their language and when a pure Hindi word is spoken before them, they say showing no curiosity about knowing its meaning- "Hindi words are out of my understanding, please make me understand in English." Just think and imagine the future. Linguistic knowledge makes man great and excretes the ability of excursion. With this point of view as much knowledge of different languages should be acquired is not only good but beneficial also. But which we made medium for this earning, seeing it with disdainful eyes is nothing but merely ungratefulness.

Readers will be surprised to read that I am writing this article in English but I am going to write something in favor of Hindi. It is because I myself am an Indian and a Hindi speaking people. I speak and write Hindi very well. It is in my blood as well as very respectful for me so it has always been first choice for me. So here I would like to do some advocacy of Hindi. This very year (2012) some months ago in South Africa a world Hindi seminar was organized at Johannesburg. The well known prudent personalities of the world and officers, ornamented with highest positions became the part of this ceremony and they very much emphasized on making Hindi the global language and publicize it all over the world. This is actually the subject of appreciation and proud for language. But with reference to this matter there is one more fact that is actually considerable- some gentle persons there who should be counted as prudent of the highest categories and who were present there as an active part of the seminar- they neither had a bit knowledge of Hindi nor they knew how to speak Hindi. But they were Indians. With reference to this matter one question is worthy of quotation- Did they accepted to be a part of this Hindi language publicity seminar as they wanted to get the universal fame? Whatever it is, but despite not having the knowledge of Hindi publicizing it seems to be as a person who is always drunk all day all night but educate others not to do this.

A national level politician is invited to address the mass assembly on the occasion of national Hindi day. Having arrived the stage the politic man starts his speech with these words- "I am very glad to be here on the great occasion of national Hindi day." Just think- on the occasion of Hindi day use of English words in his statements-perhaps it demonstrates the high class lifestyle of that Neta Ji.

In the extra copy, particularly published on Sunday, of Hindi daily news paper Amar Ujala, a poem written by a five years old little girl, was published- I don't remember the date but its heading was- "*Hindi hai mathe ki bindi*". Reading it the heart excited with delight and the mind became curious to drop itself in the golden imaginations of future. A girl merely of five and this point of view towards the mother language- it is inspirational indeed.

Today, the need is to create an interest in children for their mother tongue. Only then the existence of Hindi language which is one of the most ancient languages of the universe may be kept conserved.

I have written this article also in Hindi in my firstly written poetry essence "DYUTA KARMA PHALA". This English article is a translation for the people in India and abroad India who may not understand Hindi.

LITERARY AND MYTHOLOGICAL KNOWLEDGE

The Indian mythological literature is very deep and bottomless ocean of knowledge. There are such invaluable pearls hidden in this unlimited ocean of knowledge, if a common man get them, his life will become enriched with magnificent wealth. The need is to search them with concentrated mind and use them statutorily.

Today in India the student suppose the study of western literature more interesting as well as beneficial. They took more delight in study of Shakespeare and Milton's literature than that of Kalidasa and Vedavyasa respectively. Perhaps it is the outcome of the modernization of the society or it may also be that the study of mythological stories is supposed by them to be orthodox and superstitious. But so far as it is about modernization, then modernization can not at all mean westernization. Knowledge is free, it is completely unbounded, it is limitless, and it is quite impossible to confine it. In that case whatever literature it may be, eastern or western- study of all literatures is beneficial and knowledge improving. But the negligence of one's own mother literature and to contempt it is quite unjust and despising. Literature is the mirror of society and the mythological literature is the crown of entire literature- which provides us the understanding of our lifestyle, discipline, justice-injustice, and how to identify just-unjust and the life is enriched everyday with innovative motivations. These motivations give us energy for the predestined plans of life and the man leads to the path of evolution.

The creation of the presented piece of poetry has also been done with the object of attracting the common mass to the literary knowledge. The poetic sketch of Kauravas organized gambling yard, underlying the great Indian epic ***"MAHABHARATA"***created by Bhagwan Vedavyasa, will surely motivate the readers towards the Indian poetry and mythological literature.

With the objects which making base, this poetry part has been created, the writer is assured to achieve them with kind cooperation of readers.

2. BACKGROUND OF THE STORY

***H**aving the kind company of lord Shrikrishna Pandavas constructed the city Indraprastha and started dwelling there with their mother Kunti and wife Panchali (Draupadi). Since this grand city was got constructed by Yogamaya hence it was unique as well as full of incredible beauty. The description of its beauty and splendor was beyond the pen of learned individuals. The most beautiful cities of the world were compelled to decline their eyes before this marvelous city as the full moon, draped with milk-like white ray-collection, commences slowly-slowly to bend its head with the very first ray of the sun and in the last surrenders itself completely to the sun. Witnessing the palace, incredible, unique beautiful and lighted with millions of suns, even the presiding of heaven, the king of devas, Lord Indra was coveted to achieve it. But seeing the armor in Krishna's form on it he had to somehow satisfy himself.*

The treasury of the city Indraprastha was indeed not left from any pearl jewel or ornament of the universe. On inspecting it, it seemed to be as the god of wealth deity Kubera had entrusted the entire wealth to this treasury, gathering from the paradise and every corner of the world. To describe the origin and end of this limitless prosperity was not indeed an easy task.

The royal garden of Indraprastha was packed with trees, draped with different kind of flowers and fruits. The unique fragrance of wonderful flowers flowing in the garden, the twittering of beautiful birds glittering like gold, and the sweet humming sound of the black bees was enough to attract easily someone towards there. The large black bees would drink the juice on flowers as a tiny child was drinking the milk peacefully and fearlessly clinging to his mother's breast. Seeing the countless butterflies of different colors flying over the garden, it seemed to be as the stars of the sky could not wait for the night and began to wander here and there in the garden even in day to loot the lovely delight of the garden's beauty, descending from heaven on the earth. At the day break as soon as the feeble beams of the sun lay on pool's water in the garden, the pool seemed to be full of red rubies. And in the afternoon the forceful light of the sun made the pool packed with silver molecules. To get a single glimpse of such incredible, glorious and the beautiful empire, not only men but also the deities were coveted.

Once upon a time, Yudhishthira, motivated with the words of lord Krishna, organized Rajsuya Yagya for achieving the desired success. The Yagya was organized on the vastest level. Kings of all the empires were respectfully invited in the ceremony. As a common rule an invitation card was also sent to Hastinapur too. As an outcome Duryodhana and his maternal uncle Shakuni, the king of Gandhara state, appeared at Indraprastha to join the ceremony. Seeing the strange beauty of Indraprastha their eyes began to dazzle and the sense of jealousy commenced overflowing in the mind. After the well accomplishment of the ceremony all the kings returned to their kingdoms but Duryodhana and his maternal uncle Shakuni stayed there for visiting Indraprastha. Yudhishthira respectfully welcomed their desire and arranged their luxurious accommodation. One day Duryodhana with his uncle Shakuni walked for visiting the palace. On foregoing some steps they got a place, filled with water on surface. For proceeding safely they began to walk with raised their clothes. But no sooner did they put their first step on water than they were overwhelmed with wonder. There was no water but the shadow of water which looked like water on the surface. Both the men overwhelmed with surprise made their clothes downward and began to walk with a common pace. On walking a step or two they got a place which seemed to be completely free of water. Confused Duryodhana took a step forward thinking-if a dry place may look like full of water, then a watered place may also look like a dry place. Conflicting with these thoughts he inspected the place. His suspicion was dead and he got the place dry. Again on walking a step or two he once more found a place full of water. Sure about happening nothing unexpected both the men kept on proceeding like an intoxicated elephant. But having lay their first step into the water, the balance of their body staggered as a hut made from the feeble bamboo sticks is compelled to kiss the surface of earth, losing its balance due to the strong blow of wind. In the mean time Draupadi, visiting the palace with her lady friends, watched from attic the pitiable condition of Duryodhana and Shakuni and mocked them saying- "the son of a blind is really blind". As if an unarmed warrior is worthy to do nothing else except fluttering after a sudden attack of hundreds of arrows on his breast. The very right condition of Duryodhana was there. He was burnt with wrath and returned with Shakuni to Hastinapur with the warning to retaliate for his insult.

Since then Duryodhana began to wait for a single chance for retaliation. Shakuni told duryodhana that it was not only hard to defeat Pandavas in battle but also impossible. So they can only be defeated by tactic not power. He suggested Duryodhana to invite Pandavas to Hastinapur for playing stake. He also assured him that having conquered the stake he could not only retaliate for his insult but also he could be the master of bottomless and splendid property of Indraprastha. Since Shakuni was a skillful player of gambling and his enchanted dices always obeyed him. Being motivated by shakuni Duryodhana invited Pandavas to Hastinapur and organized an assembly for playing stake, which has been depicted in this poetry essence.

3. HASTINAPUR

1. Senate of Duryodhana, some special organize
Nay know it's casual or deeply pre-planned
The court is boiling with the water of wise-
And forceful valiant and warriors armed

2. The prime seat covered by the man unsighted
King of the state looks too helpless
Sink in false love of cunning Infrighted[1]
Son knows nothing of curse and bless

3. The chair is lighting with glory of great-
Bhagirathi's son[2] *on a point of court*
Bhishma well known the maker of fate
Valliant victor straighten throat[3]

4. The battle expert, genius, the great coach of war
In face of Drona, Almighty bowed their head
Seated in the court where above they are
At an end with grave in the chair's bed

5. The learned Ethician[4] *with unbeatable seat*
Seated Kripacharya the one in all

Every corner of that daring street[5]
Flowing over there with heroic rain fall[6]

6. In a row of that very court of polite-
Policies of vidura are lighting with light-
Of knowledge glowing the great and bright
The whole country Aryavarta day and night

7. Who is erudite in the congress of huge?
Than great vidura and who is more-
Worthy bow taker as Arjuna. Reduce
Proud of each, Karna's donation store[7]

8. Uncountable such individuals became the part-
Of great Kuruvansha[8] *but oh! Ill fate*
Some of them were too sweet heart
Some of them were devil's mate

9. Marvelous phylum now a history on pages-
Of futurity. O GOD! The great ocean of-
Bravery knowledge though a land of sages
Still converted into yama's loaf[9]

10. Axis of the court a quadrant stage
Right in front the throne of the king
Not others but some familiar face

Team like ready for some sport in the ring

11. At an end smiling the pentagon[10] with light
Some thirsty eyes of greed are raining the rains-
Of resentment. In the middle such goods in sight
As a game of stake is created in brains

12. Curiosity evident on every witnessed face
Struggling and battling some pre-familiar bodies
With emotions of optimist or pessimistic case
O GOD! Will they be thralled by shameless fraudies[11]?

13. What turn will take today the play of stake
Otherwise a fierce battle it will make
Between two brothers for monarchy's sake
It seems to be a war of true and fake

14. Voracious Duryodhana hath taken the aim
Blatant view of shakuni hath captured the game
Days some earlier he uttered some name
Enemies will be thralled with thee get the fame

15. Do game plan as I have mastered
It. Nay be anxious we follow thy good
Years I passed in dice gambled
Then hath found that art touch wood!

16. Let me show thee, the gambler's stake
The Pandavas will dance on fingers tip
Remember O dear neph[12]! The goal thee make
Thy honor is Draupadi's honor's strip

17. If forget in Indraprastha a bolt from the blue
The proud lady made us how much fun?
Fun of then here payback will do
All will be thralled besides no one

18. Thoughts of yours Oh! I never misbrained[13]
Beating them all for the taste of winning
Then the chatty women pitiably restrained
Mute eyes will caste on the game of cunning

4. THE CHAUSAR BEGINS

19. The Stake started with dancing of dices
A great war also on chausar's base[14]
Jyeshtha and shakuni now face to face
Oh! Stake is draped with betraying slices

20. Stakes one or two conducted to amuse
Winnings exchanging the place in turn
Moments gone some in simplest fun
Humpty shots darted for some time to use

21. Hours passed in and the prince impatient
Uttered - the small stakes art out of fun
O brat! Shoot big with adventures gun
Open thyself in stakes battlement

22. Weapons too fatal now raised in battle-
Of gambling stage. As duryodhana's craze
Wagers large over the gambling barge
Probable impact as a real fact

23. By Shakuni's cun[15]*dices of fun*
Shown in the court of the grandest fort

Result he wished which never he missed
The time hath come he thought day some

24. Pandavas ignorant from the betray behind-
The back. They were untouched entire
Keeping enthralled more than prior
Untied and banded themselves they find

25. The wealth they got with glory so far
Putting on stakes again and again
In hope of return in hope of gain
Each and every of theirs they mar

26. Splendid citadel of the land paradise
As kubera's[16]*revenue thicken with gold-*
And silver's orns[17]*and new gems hold*
Army chaturaangini's[18]*power too nice-*

27. With pacing steed and trumpet alouds
And chariots incredible and pawns on land
Conquered duryodhana with easy hand
His soul now floating in colding clouds

28. Each surprised and face melancholised
The Pandavas five now gone in the strive
How happen so bad O God! How sad!

It's a trap no doubt what gain of shout

29. We lost our all at the edge of fall
If cry to repent for no amendment
The bird hath flown from the cage of own
Will never return each man here stun

30. Then the tongue of son of crowned monarch
Uttered some words are savage at all
Tolerable to no which lifeless you call
Words distressing and full of dark

31. Thou lost thy all thee depart with what?
Show thy face how number of mass?
Thy sincere subject thy social gross
Tell me O brat[19]! With broken heart

32. Thou beggar of path what pair with me
I won Indraprastha thou turned ordinary
From worldly empire's monarch so dreary
Am victor of dices' war but thee-

33. A knight of lose of defeat at all
Thee nothing for me except I tweet
Merely the beauty of walking street-
Steps of mine brat O! what a fall!

34. Yet myself thyself each others
Cousins no doubt we are by heart
Intentionally therefore thee honor's part
For the sake of Younger and elder brothers

35. I got my win thou found thy loss
Say embarrassment –" go thy home"
I pour a chance as a ray in the gloam
May thou get all with a final toss

5. THE PROPOSAL AND DILEMMA

36. Everything I victed will put on stake
Return the wholest for a single bet
Dices if liked thou art become mate-
Of glorious winning then save to break

37. Listen me however it's not so easy
Put on Stake some extraordinary
Out of wealth apparent thy summary
So put thy bro[20]*on stake hopefully*

38. Let thy brain consider in deep
The final toss of the final bet
Previously lost if nothing will get
An attempt may take thee to honor's heap

39. Why so mute as silence for what?
Even residue of hope will go from hands
Of returning the wealth and loosing the bands
So break the ice nay someone's heart

40. As a mighty watered and full of flood
Ocean hath thrown a lovely fish
From its lap outside upon the land
As a parrot's consort passing its days
Wordless and soundless sitting in cage
In detachment of its lovely spouse

❧❧❧

41. As a weary wingy distressed creature's[21] *mind*
Thinks to go back and returning home
Finding no way but water's flow
Of endless eternal O God! Infinite
Sea, sea's power aft miles and miles
Flying over the blue and hopeless entire

❧❧❧

42. As a black bird[22] *looking for a pitcher and flying-*
To and fro with dry throat
As black long creeper[23] *hath lost its gem*[24]
And surviving in the only hope to get it
As a tiny frog isth ensnared by hoody snake
In its deadly hold despite attempting a lot-
Looks alone and entirely unaided
To himself, its time's impact my friends!

❧❧❧

43. What's it? O God! The crooked play of dices-
Or whirl of time. What a mockery! Indeed
A lord of numberless innumerable slaves
Isth going to be slave Alas! Himself
Considered each moral way but got dead end

The lord of religion[25] finally, compelled for the bet last

44. Words announced to surrender the bro
On altar of gambling stunned the whole mass
Embarrassment aroused to catch everyone
What a crush of morality! In the court despite-
Thicken with bravery. And restless minds
Witnessed all but nay speak a word

45. How disdainful game! which brought the men-
Away from amity but at daggers dawn
Native relative of own forfeit for trivial trashy and full of shame-
Shabby sport which you say the stake
O creator! Thou turned this royal, descendant to the way of ruin
Ganga's son hath broken the chair in this conflict of mind with self

46. Oft such events are unprivileged
If time oppose the fate goes to enmity
Next is what? If think went on-
Thinking with restless and confuse minds
In the ocean of thoughts deep and wide
Dives of emotions being taken by them

47. Now recommencing the crazy play, the black time-
Of Pandava's life and unanticipated
Breaking the limits of decency Oh! The tricky web of dices
Trying to overcome the puzzle of heart Yudhishthira the Ex. Emperor-

Of glorious Indraprastha uttered some words
To chuck dices with only and last willing of almighty God

48. A man of painless, patient and polite emotions
Moreover gentleness of heart and freshness in nature
Sahedeva's at obedience peak worshipable brotherhood
Not a bit intervention for the sake of his brother's faith
Gleely received his own sacrifice
In only hope of back to home with honor

49. As Shakuni tried to draw the game more
Bhishma's emotion's pot blasted at once
A sudden sound echoed over there and then
It made the palace buzzed when great Ganga's son
Stood up like a steady strong and long-lasting tree
Pronouncing a single word- hey stop!

50. Getting down the glorious seat he explained
The throned monarch of the game of today-
Is no how apt to the justice code
Sport is what boosts amity's power-
And emotions and makes the harmless time
A source of humor and mental amusement

51. Howth crooked game and what a sport of wonder!
Where decency hath no values really my lord!
Is a crisis of humanity the fact no doubt.

Nay sow the seeds hostile and do the game over
Create a history here the new and wondrous
Returning them back to their royal prosperity

52. If nay my lord! The royal kingdom of-
Hastinapur will go to ruin I say its firm
And the man you say Bhishma is really tortured
With the only thought of dispute in the court
Say thy son O great lord! To cease from here-
The pungent play and repent the ill words uttered

53. O dear Duryodhana! Give up persistency on thy part my son!
And embrace the words of Pitamaha's think
They are truth's notice Brahma's black and white
Thy ill deeds out of religion will lead the phylum whole-
To the edge of ruin. This man unsighted ill fate! ill fate!
How save the kingdom from deadly crisis

54. Valliant dread of fate but never
None but their arms power overcomes the fate
The whole prosperity n all their lust
Conquered by me nay got in alms
The course was free at all voluntary
Exerted the game aft cousin's consent

55. I hold emulation and each one ailed
Duryodhana overcame it's a brutal sin

Nay push me away off desired goal
Victory hath come right in my hands
Its game my friends! My friends! My friends!
Rules are made here but once

56. Shakuni drives his dices on path of plain
And a horse-laugh sound buzzed at once
Ah! It was Duryodhana's bursting in laugh
Next moment Yudhishthira got painful realize
My piece of heart O God! O fate!
Now demon's slave now demon's slave

57. it's my calamity or Duryodhana's chance
Or God's write or duplicity unknown
Hath nothing to say hath nothing to heed
Confused of stepping to the mother's door
With four of us she born us five
She is mother of us the mother of five

58. Be better if I exert once more
With all me too will dwell in slavery
Hath lost my all whether big or little
In the blatant play of dices even-
The dearest for me in the world my bro
Hath become a slave he used to be lord

59. Hath nothing to lose as vanished each all

Outstanding the wreath of Krishna's name
With three of mine let's take a more step
With Krishna's name he sighed full sore
Put my all bodies on stake
As my dear bro now come what may

60. Either we get all or lose even body's skin
But never leave a chance to blame on us
By upcoming days he thought with heart
Determining the mind the Ex. great lord
Uttered the prince to commence the play
With anxious nervous and keen thought spheres

6. HARD DESCISIONS

61. Let's see the gain of gambling play
The witch of dices terrific today
The Black God's time[26] couldn't help in even
The black time of their career's way

62. Moment to moment they all brothers four
Lined mutually together over more
The lord of religion himself obliged
To sit in losers with mental sore

63. The lions- even tiny overthrow never faced
Ah! Circumstances! Thy cruelties art great
Thee made them now as a dispersed streak
Thee made them as all men them hate

64. The twang of bow whose gracious presence
Symbolize his magnificent amazing entrance
The valiant bow taker the Kunti's son
Is caged today by the rare circumstance

65. The mace star Bheemsena wondrous might
Deca thousand beasts' art nothing in fight

With long-long trunks and heavy strengthen-
Column-Like feet and heavens height

66. Sitting bowed head as a beautiful flower-
Got abandoned it hath no power
Oft it played and swing with bough
In the wood unbanned at desired hour

67. The five in the court assembled unease
With adjectival bodies of theirs art freeze
Holding the only note omnipresent
Why stake O friends! It mars it's a craze

68. Stake, heed O world! Is nothing my friend!
But a sabotage in life and tyranny's trend
Mar men's life some same is today
Mute sound uproar the all head bend

69. Meanwhile Duryodhana the prince of state
Mocked them all same time same date
Tried to do them affronting act
Full of disgust and full of hate

70. Thou wereth king, what doubt, too good
Better servant thou art Touch wood!
Change is the Nature's steady rule

It's true it's fact today thou proved

❧❧❧

71. Nay slur instant the royal attire
It's ungood so now thy limbs stir
And take them off thy royal touch
Sense of slavery thee please acquire

❧❧❧

72. In a casual situation I can understand
Anguish apparent when someone in band
The world is delusion's grandest home
Sitting chuckles someone moaning stand

❧❧❧

73. One chance is left my brother! If think
With colden head with zero shrink
Can back thy pleasant hours once more
Play another stake take loses' drink

❧❧❧

74. May get a chance still last and late
To prove thyself to test thy fate
In the game thee hath completely lost
The residue of honor to save O brat!

❧❧❧

75. The marvelous palace of mine with glory-
Of Indraprastha. As in angle's story-
Heaven's woods where golden wings
Fly over there with lovely twittery

76. The splendid throne set with jewel-
Gems and orns[27] garnished with pearl
All thou won what hath to me?
Nay me my bros but hopes art null

77. Wealth incredible thy great and grand
Though is reserved in my command
A beautiful pearl oh! Yet is left
Wondrous uncosted[28] and safe new brand

78. The gem which is left hath witless cost
The heaviest of all the gems thee lost
Press thy wit to think my wish
The consort of five the lady of boast

79. Who then hear stunned with fear
Faces fade as roses dead
Then Bhīma's brain could not restrain
Of self terrified the flames inside

80. Oh man abject! With shameless project
Thy dismal propose I strictly oppose
In thy prig view the honor is a new-
Gem like thing of the lady of a king

81. Hold thy tongue hey! Man thou art-
A slave merely not an army's part
Doth thee recall nay the fact worldwide?
Duryodhana the great is master of thy heart

82. Beware! If not thou hold thy rage-
As thunder's roar in the cloud's cage
Thou'll find thy head on land no qualm
Fluttering away from body's stage

83. Do chat some words, O religion's lord!
Nay waste the time in the time hard
Open the cage of thy gracious fangs
Take some decision in the gambling yard

84. If thy wealth thou want to return
All thy brothers with citadels fun
The only move which you can take
Draupadi's stake will hath to be done

85. Protest a lot but duryodhana fearless
Not hear a word from any's face
Obstinacy's craze did not let him do
To follow others restraining the pace

86. The devil desire he got inside-
The psyche acquiring Draupadi's pride
Taking revenge to crush pathetic
Trample the honor of royal bride

87. Who can I show my coerce in deep
Who can I call to serve my weep?
Who the almighty can I contemplate
Who can help me in crisis of my grief?

88. Oh dear spouse! For the cruel deed
Let me hath thy for the false creed-
Of mine in the circumstances array
Now taking decision uncommon unfreed

89. The prince impatient uttered at once
To dear maternal not miss the chance
Plunder compensation of the game instant
Crafted for what aft a lengthy penance

90. Then stroke in the last awful terrible
As a deadly assault fatal too horrible
A deep dark spread in front of the eyes
A sudden blow of adamant's bundle

7. BEYOND THE CRUELTY

91. The victor Duryodhana forthwith recall
Pratikami[29] the man with a spear tall
Ordered to take the lady now a maid
In front of me in the gambling hall

92. Send her the order avoiding delay
Appear at the court at the time at the day
To serve sincerely some royal deeds
The lady at once on the spot of the play

93. Hath wasted a huge amount of time
For the one n only chance of prime
Then a camel's hump approached underneath-
The vastest mount[30] the prince then rhyme

94. Who abused my honor I recall
Facing her friends on my sudden fall
I too'll strip her royal repute .
Facing ministers and guests as a doll

95. Hours some passed and the man with spear
Returned with reply from Pandavas dear-

Lady of five uttered- what a mock!
Howth royal bride to the court can walk

96. With no aim she said the men in the court
Along with the prince the royal's port
Forget I think the way to invite
In decent exertion the imperial bride

97. As somebody made a lethal stroke
With a healthy pole on serpent's yoke
Vomiting the fire the prince an ounce
Of dirty ill words as below he pronounce

98. The frail fragile lean slender infirm
Lady absurd not more than the term-
A beggar's spouse mutuals her place
With royal family's women's grace

99. The witless opposite of male so dare
Throw my orders flow in spare
Who made all her fives royal servant
Censure his thoughts the lady indignant

100. Now see my lady the inviting's way
Send you the message eccentric today
Rebuke of the rashness on thy part

Pay you back in a manner smart

101. Dushashana![β1] you leave at once and go
Fetch her forthwith my loving Bro!
If show retaliation or a bit storms
Catch her to draw with forceful arms

102. Heed my words to get conclusion
Hold her curly strings to drag-on-
Land. That body's half shouldst touch
Running on part of earth as much

103. The time when Dushashana Duryodhana's Bro
Left the majestic assembly's main door
Silence melancholies as cemetery sphere
Draped for a while meantime over there

104. Clouds of queries start thatching over-
The place in the sky of court so poor
Queries unseen were moving around
Seeking perfection but hardly they found

❦❦❦

105. Moment of then the morality's crown
Hath broken the ice the light of the town
His truthful tongue words tried to create
Howth royal family's astonishing ill fate!

106. His restless ogles then began to rain
With tears of disquiet with tears of pain
Hardly couldth say a word two four
His weary lips hath exhausted more

107. Seeking courage he drove his tongue
With a little pace in the people among
To show the pain in heart of own
Not rapidly but prompted the moan

108. In the royal state, he said, of ours
Women are seen as own mothers
There the bride of palace with honor
Treated with too much disdainful dishonor

109. In the mean time Karna brighten his fact
Duryodhana's deed is a loyal act
A lady with many is nature's blur
Honor dishonor is nothing to her

110. She hath the pleasure of nights alone
Not with one but several known
What should be told to the lady about?
Known as a slut in the culture no doubt

111. Arrows of words with bearless dart
From bow of tongue dissecting the heart
Pinched the inner conscience as though
Millions of swords art piercing the soul

112. The heart inflamed it began to burn
Gathering the blaze some patience they earn
The Gandeeva Arjuna's deadly bow
And Bhima's mace is steady in the row

113. Aft my friends! At exertion's place
A scene of event awkwardly displays
Slander shame and malice themselves
Surrender them before those cruel wolves

114. A hefty man with shameless dare
Dragging caught a feeble woman's hair
Cries of pains art buzzing the whole
Dignity's castle and gambling court-

115. Aft moments some passed he jerked her
To the cruelty's lord his own brother
Thinking some thoughts who gave his brain
A sudden jolt again and again

116. The greatest affront I ever tolerate
In state Indraprastha here retaliate
Oh! sluts' queen thy turn of cry
As I let you sit now on my thy

117. Draupadi arrived at assembly hall
Rotated her view around the wall
None looked her with straighten eyes
No one couldth dare ask why she cries

118. Apart from a young prince of the state
Known as Vikarna is beyond the hate
Younger of Duryodhana the devil's mate
Yet in decency he is forward straight

119. This is injustice this is cruelty
This is somewhat affronting morality
Oh my brother! It's a deed of offence
Slur like that with a lady's reference

120. Listen and look O seniors! Senators!
Teacher preachers and kingdom creators
Oh! Come ahead somebody from the mass
For honors' sake which a lady's gross

121. Stop it! O witless! The tribe's rebel

Getting enmity to whom you scoundrel!
If thy wit hath gotth unawared
Duryodhana's relation with thee yet dared!

122. Whose honor here thou trying to save
Appealing to all here sitting with grave
Spouse of who's in a current compete
Lost her, himself in a gambling beat

123. The discourse stopped by prince by prince
Panchali started to say mute since
Going to each in the justice court
One by one for mental support

124. Bhishma and Drona and Pandavas five
Every human in the senate civilize
No one coudth dare to match one's eyes
With the lady alone who really surprise

125. The surrendered heads were asked by her
With a question disclosed in disappointed manner
Which how reply and who who know
The query was indeed logical though

126. In a play of stake she inquired of all
Who lost himself and agreed thrall

Who offered him right, to play bet again?
The next stake is a foolish insane

127. She couldth get mere silence and mute
For the query stable hath no repute
Ailed with ail for attempt sterile
As no one she found standing in the trial

128. I realize in the warriors' crowd
No one is left valiant with proud
Who hath in the case arrows with power
Nay rain blaze at least some shower

129. The time then Duryodhana again would pass-
An order to him of the most wicked class
Rob the attire of the lady acute
Who tried to rob my precious repute

130. Instantly approached to Draupadi's dress
Snatching as a lion famished of flesh
On deer's dear so feeble and soft
Running to-fro with hopeless heart

131. Seeking the path of defense in the hall
Around the royal citadel's each wall
Ah cruel fate! It what thee done

Leave no chance to defend even one

132. As a brutal body in eagle's form
Chases a feathered feminine's arm
She weeps perplexed puzzled unease
He burst in laughter blatantly tease

133. Her mind stuck abruptly with a thought
A ray in the dark suddenly she got
No one to me in the dark worldwide
Only you Krishna the lord of bride

134. Every way, hindered in the castle's cage
Of my dead life please listen my prays
Commenced invoking dear lord of hers
Begging for help in the time of curse

135. The ache displayed of the lady alone
With sodden eyes and painful moan
Shaky doors of jaws more bent
Muttering the Krishna's name frequent

136. For honors sake I put with calm
My honor O Krishna! On thy palm
Doth thee recall love thread I truss? -
On thy arm please save it to crush

137. Do you hear O Krishna! My lord!
My call of compassion the universal God
Sensation of mine the whole consciousness-
Of soul in a fix by fear's stress

138. Need you I seek me entirely alone
In array which made from molesters' bone
In complications web at situations wall
Thoughts take rise but suddenly fall

139. If not caste thy eyes of kind
On thy sist if you see behind
The world will curse O descent of God
Thou as well thy sayings a lot

140. When justice injustice hold a fight
Every moment religion is bright
But ill duty of theirs' will attest
Religion is merely a short time guest

141. She saw abruptly keeping consider
Devil Dushashana approaching to her
Stop it! Tyrant the autocrat task
Hold thy body wear shy's mask

142. A lady devoted to spouse's adore
Hath chastity's power nay dare to roar
Penalty of yours will be bearing all
Don't do such dare O sinful tall

8. THE DISDAINFUL ATTEMPT

143. Stop thy trashy chats and craze
Baseless vain thee show me the rage
Creators blunder O lady! unwise
Worry thyself and coming up cries

144. Who is to come to face my sword?
To make a defense of thee in the court
Who hath valor to build thy save
From gallant Dushashana's arm's cave

145. Duryodhana and all his devil mates
Commenced exciting his body's weights
Pushing him more and more and more
For shameful dis-action[32] full of abhor

146. Do her exposed Duryodhana uttered
And Let me squeeze this fairy bird
Explain the fact to lady of day dream
Mock of Duryodhana isth costly extreme

147. The act of shame, doing manhood defame
The cruel ill deed, isth nameless indeed
Snatching esteem, of mother's scream
Human civilize in the court of dice

148. Then Why imps, let's have a glimpse
Art not good than, those civil court's man
They never do brides, but serve with prides
In court wearless, to strip their dress

149. O God! Toil defame, in future's frame
Shouldst never repeat, in any street
O God almighty! This time's variety
Shouldst nay come again, it pours too pain

150. Who is the doer, of the doing poor?
Who doth endure, its result mature
O readers! It's none, but the gain of fun
Of dice's playing, it's Mishra's saying

151. Now heed my words, the game is a curse
The rest and peace, it snatches and tease
The tiny love faces, with smiling blesses
Art cruelly run down, by gambling's frown

152. Apples of eyes, themselves deprive

Mother's sons, they get separations
Brides in the game, illfull and damn
Ruin their dream, of golden stream

153. The Gambler stands, and washed his hands
Off wealthy world, and got hurled
Outside the folk, and a laughing stock-
Becomes and lose, his vanity's gross

154. World see him, in moments grim
With disdainful eyes, and full of surprise
To walk with raised, head dazed
The hardest thing, for whole living

9. A SHAMEFUL SCANDAL

155. Same in the hall, thicken with gall
The five strengthy, valorous and healthy-
Men head down, watching the sound-
Of shameful scandal, of consort mutal

156. Warriors others, with five brothers
Helplessness displays, on perplexed face
Thinking- O God! Send me abroad
Or give me death, ere death of faith

157. Complications a lot, hurricane of thoughts
Exploitation caught, exploited heart
Explosion too mean, of bearless scene,
Scattered the mass, as dispersed straws

158. Done by one, tis work stun
All hath wet, the lenses set
O reader! It's none, but the gain of fun
Of dice's playing, it's Mishra's saying

159. Grasped the saree's end of hers
Started to draw as five brothers

And senators in hall their wetted eyes-
Closing themselves as someone cries

160. Instigating Duryodhana instantly to him
Screaming loudly with immodest grim
Draw her cloth my bro Oh no!
Pain apparent on lady's brow

161. When she knew herself entirely-
Unable to do attempt even only
Raised the hands to the heaven's side
Muttering the names for Krishna's guide

162. Nay do delay means please do haste
O flute reciter nay time waste
A woman's call a woman's sob
A woman's honor probably rob

10. DRAUPADI'S PRAYER

HINDI POEM

163. Hey! Madhusudana Nandlal hey yashudanad dularey
Hey murlidhar varshneya brij ki ankho ke tarey
Hey Brijbhushan jagatvibhushan Natwar nandkishore
Hey Govinda hey Gopala natkhat makhanchor

164. Damodara O chakrapadmdhara Gopivallabha swami
vasudeva shriKrishnachandra hey Shridhara antaryami
Gopeshwara hey Jagdishwara Vrindavanalal Bihari
Girdhara Nagara Keshava Madhava Shridayala Banvari

165. Hey Janardana Banshiwale Kanha Deenadayala
Naaganathaiya Rasarachiya Shyama Tribhangilala
Deenabandhu Sankathari Suradeva Dwarikadheesha
Janvallabh Ghanshyam Ramapati jai jai Shri Jagdeesha

166. Kamalnayana Gopriya Suresha hey Padmnabha Bhayahari
Radheshyama Sadasukhakari hey Govardhanadhari
Bhagatvasal Kamalapati shri Hari Shri Sarvaswa Sujana
Hey Sukhasagara hey Brijanagara Shri Shri Kripanidhana

167. Parmanandama Gopichandama shrish Devkinandana
Omkara Narayana Swami Shesh shayine vandana
Dayasindhu O Chakrapani O vishwadhar niranjana
Radharamana Sant Anuragi sada sarvadukhabhanjana

168. O Brijesha O Rishikesha Bhavbhanjana Ghat-Ghatvasi
O Karunanidhi Kunj bihari O Shripati Avinashi
O Kripalu ab Kripa Karo Sankat Se Mujhe Ubaro
Brijkishore O Madanmurari bhavsagar se Taro

11. THE MIRACLE AND THE CURSE

169. Against the strong Will of whose
Not a single leaf can move a bit
He who doth not exist if,
The survivals can never exist

170. He who lies in the each particle
In conscious unconscious in dead or alive
In mountain's height in air's flow
In every moment with land and sky

171. In the grand supremacy of Almighty-
God, if something occurs misfortunate
Humanity will lose, will drop forever
From God its true and ancient faith

172. But he who trust in might's great power
With mind and heart with true and pure
The almighty Krishna always stands
For honors sake it's true it's sure

173. Panchali started to meditate Krishna
With silent sense again and again
To demolish the woe in the deep woe betide-
Of CHEERHARANA[33] which bursting the brain

174. Emerged right then the God with flute
As a power invisible for men unseen
The happening occurred was beyond the thought
Marveled the whole mass too keen

175. The more he tried to spend his power
To draw her clothes to make her strip
The more it kept spreading its length
It's no merely cloth but god's firm grip

176. The marvel beyond the limits of marvel
What a marvelous scene! Marveled the all
Duryodhana looks too intoxicated
Knowing his aim is going to fall

177. The cloth hath wrapped up the lady's orth[35]
The lady herself isth the running cloth
Beyond the limit of one's intellect
The question is the heaviest everyone's forth

178. A long strip of cloth, mentioned above

Quintals of cloths a heap like makeup
Started gathering rapidly at once
As it was making a mountains cup

179. The man of energy hath soon become-
The powerless fellow in moments few
Couldn't do he wanted to make her strip
But a man of character's fall he grew

180. Wearied so badly he fell on the earth
As a tree incised with lacking strength
And hopes to live he knows so well
That now he's unable to secure his birth

181. He fell unconscious with the miracle inside-
The glorious court was well accomplished
The troop of honesty was highly content
And devil spirits but had a chide

182. Contentment sighed with a feel of content
She uncovered the eyes from curtains of lids
Then her wits came to have a feel of relax
Ere some hours was a prey apparent

183. The lady spoke- she hath no ail at all
Why doth she do hesitation the least?

As they are the men neither man nor woman
What to hope them for a shelter's call

184. As a group of hare captured in jackals'-
Blatant trap they do baseless appeal
As cruel, kindless and beyond the mercy
Feline bodies, for rats enthralls

185. Assassin beast hath no tend but to slay
To take life only with callous heart
Hence throng should have expectations but why?
From deadly beasts no more no way.

186. I too offended, the heaviest of all
That asked for wealth to previously vagrant
Like asking fruits delicious and sweet
At massless woods from thorned tall

187. But heed my words O Kshatriyas[34] black sheep!
Boasting for Kshatritwa[35] thou all in the court
Displaying thy force of shameful might
By confining a she[36] into stratagem heap

188. The one accused of making impious
Until nothing but sow his corpse-
Into dust and wash my untied hair

With crimson blood of the rogue of vice

189. The meeting of hair must not at all-
Be Held herein well, whether I die
It's a vow firmly taken by none-
But a Kshatriya's lady, will never fall

190. O Handful tyrannies and bunch of crooks
Thee hath done the sin an unforgiving
The grand this city is now about to hang
On dark clouds of disaster's hooks

191. The doing isth yours but the whole countrymen
Of the city well known Hastinapur the great
Will directly bear with the tough penalty
The king or saints or other than none

192. Blasted from the lips of mine wretched face
A single utterance will no away go waste
As a influence of my big infallible curse
All will go to the ruin and trash

192. The planets, the sun, the stars in the sky
The moon in the night art all my witness
Looking straight to the broadening and vast
The armor of earth and infinitely high

193. The water, the ocean, the lotus and the all-
That moved, unmoved each living in the world
Listen! A Kshatrani harassed by owns
Isth going to do a curse's call

12. THE FINAL TRAP

194. Readers! I fancy, if there some sinister
Wereth being dropped by Draupadi's lips
The raw dust pot of the royal Hastinapur-
Would break into parts and particles nips

195. Which you think frail when becomes sturdy
The globe entirely trembles with fear
The tender mimosa which dies to touch
It soonest becomes a prickly pear

196. The world is standing as an impartial witness
If injustice ever tried to be crossed
From its narrow limits then great goddess Durga
Isth formed into Kaali to slay wickedness

197. But a sudden sound of thundering shrill
Appeared at once and stopped that flow-
Of flowing river's water of rage
Approaching to them for nothing but to kill

198. The semi-blinded lady wasth no one else
Than mother of Duryodhana- on ambitions peak

Their doings will be fined by the God's great hands
She tried draw her back with the words she tells

199. Why shouldst thou now want to meet?
With stigma of ruin of the whole dynasty
The lifelong gain of thy selfless pray
Will go for nothing with a single beat[37]

200. And these silly bodies have lost their wits
Intoxication of rule doth know what of-
A woman's ail? They think each one
Mere hunting practice and game of bets

201. But now in today thou realizes nay
What offence wasth given by thee?
She gave thee gift, of life and birth
Nine full moons her blood thee pay

202. The chest of king on the highest throne
Had to face a shaft from queries case
Was drafted from Draupadi's bow of tongue
When found him doing not even a moan

203. O king of the kings of state of the states
Isth nay the duty of your states rule
To discriminate creation of justice injustice

The right and wrong in somebody's traits

204. Break the ice now O great father
And quench the thirst of boiling queries
If it wereth the bride of your own
Would have been treated with same bother?

205. I am not the own but what of the fact?
An active part of the state I am
Will all city women be treated likewise?
Here with mine of impudence perfect

206. Apologies my child apologies my child
Ashamed he uttered on all my doings
Constrained in the destiny obscured of mine
A burden to earth no light even mild

207. Unable to fill, O my dear daughter!
Disgraceful deed at my named place
But make a promise for thy kind wish
If thy wish can ask to me whatever

208. In prince's words the women's spell
Nay get trapped my adorable father
It's why that wicked lady is conquered-
By me by rules of the play done well

209. It's a dream here to liberate thyself
From my forced arms property of mine
Uttered the prince but beating with tap
His thigh in the right as a hungry wolf

210. It is beyond the limit and Bhīma aware
For naked dance of lame tendencies
Am going to have a vow unbreakable
Will do more nothing than an act of dare

211. At the final reckoning of the last held war
Dushashana's traitor dictator breastplate
Will cleave it and drink the crimson fluid
And wash the spouse's hair no far

212. Horrible tone resounds, the palace entire
Even world entire's with sound's roar
Creatures entirely then trembled with fear
Flames wereth frank of terror's fire

213. The vow one more wasth taken too
By Bhima's tongue in the flame of rage
Will fract the thigh of prince Duryodhana
A day an arena will surely do

214. King horrified and blind with fear
Attempted to tempt Draupadi's brain
Take boon my child from my humble hands
A treasure divine to you very dear

215. Enslaved by the spell of stake's whirlpool
The lord of religion my so called consort
Let me beg to you if you say
Award of his, liberation's tool

216. Granted my child which you asked for
Still my soul's desire is half done
The blind lord of this royal state-
Is willfully fain to give some more

217. Let the weary heart have some pace-
Of peace, ask me for some you desire
Something with the quality which can repay-
The luster hath passed from thy dear face

218. Do you know dear father a woman's luster
On woman's face is sloppy with none
But when its honor is trampled in pride
No water of wealth can wash it faster

219. Well dear king! If you are firm
To give some more then let me have
The state of mine with four great lords
Say, can you now fulfill your term?

220. All will be awarded to thee as reward
Thy chariot thy jewel s thy state thy kings
If thee hath inward some else
Ask for contentment now me thy guard

221. O father! My soul will be contented now
By arms ten of five lords
Heard the men in court then shouted
O wow! O wow! O wow! O wow!

222. Perplexed with piercing, Shakuni and the prince
Of the cunning plan and full of diplomacy
Uttered to the king and other men of court
With newly strategy and breaking dins

223. The wealth conquered by the sharp intellect-
Of mine. If goes it all in vain
Why one would fancy for nothing for none
The privilege of victory and about subject

224. But accepting inwardly the kind capitulation

To the words invaluable of my dear father
Prepared I am to pay them back
The wealth entire and the whole nation

225. But still would make a cordial appeal
To the rival king of mine, of play
Won't he be a laughing stock?
If he beg to get this deal

226. So I am wished, a proposal to say
A new should be played with changing rules
One who goes, to victory acquire
Gets wealth all being king of the day

227. And one who goes away from conquest
Will go to woods for not less than-
Years twelve will dwell in exile
With banishment of one to hide for test

228. If thou lost this final stake
And return herein with accomplished make
Get thy sure wealth kingdom's lake
Live with pride my words unfake

229. Yudhishthira received with friendly intention
The proposal latest of native rivals

But O cruel destiny! What thee did?
Defeated thee them previously mention

13. THE TRAGEDY

230. The emperors five of Monopoly Empire
Indraprastha and sixth the lady prior
Will turn into sages and go retire
To roam to-fro in the woods entire

231. They'll give up their luxurious life
Realizing hut with the lovely wife
No glee now of relish and rife-
Dishes but roots and only strife

232. The luxury infinite of slaves and maids
The cheerful glory of their states
The breezy incense of gardens' traits
Departing all their love and hates

233. The time is left behind they sleep-
On velvet beddings sound and deep
The time is now over straws heap
Nights with threats of lions' beep

234. The paths of pebbles and lying stones
Will try to feel so tender with moans

Her light-light foots in curious tones
Birth entangled in such woe cones-

235. How tenderness would get rid herself
Pain unendurable of the innocent elf
And forceful rain from glaring shelf
No valiant can check or help

236. Wet moans driven from the ogle streams
Of tenderness humble as fountain beams
Drenching the whole though heart screams
Earth which one's own shelter one dreams

237. Its own relations threw a deadly assault-
Of betray on us for no other fault
They formed an array for making a halt
In wealthy life for stumbles exalt

14. THE MESSAGE

238. The royal empire of greater than greats
Vanished with draughts of snub and hates
Arrows uncountable they bore on chests
Of common subject's taunting sets

239. The weal of those were certain kings
The victor of world and all the wings
Ruined and we all just ordinary things
Few than fewer against them bings [38]

240. The fake stake isth an ocean of kills
With deep infinite and limitless fills
The slight ignorance can sink to the rill-
Of no other way but the death's hill

241. Oh! Therefore one humble appeal
The ignorant poet with a great deal-
Of love and affection to make you feel
The gain of stake isth woe nay weal

WORD AID

*1.**Infrighted**- One dreads of none*

*2. **Bhagirathi's son**- Bhishma Pitamaha, a well known warrior of the great epic Mahabhharata*

*3. **Straightenthroat**- sitting with Grave and proud.*

*4. **Ethician**- One who he has deep knowledge in moral science.*

*5. **Daring street**- The court filled with brave warriors.*

*6. **Heroic rain fall**- The court is brimming with great heroes.*

*7. **Karna's donation store**- In Indian mythology karna is supposed to be the greatest donator in the world.*

*8. **Kuruvansha**- The family of Kauravas.*

*9.**Yama's loaf**- Yama is the Hindu God of death so the phrase means "got to death".*

*10. **Pentagon**- Five Pandava brothers.*

*11. **Fraudies**- Fraud persons.*

*12. **Neph**- Nephew, sister's son.*

*13. **Misbrain**- To let something go from the mind.*

*14. **Chausar's base**- gambling material same as ludo game.*

*15. **Cun**- Cunning.*

*16. **Kubera**- Kubera is a Hindu God of wealth.*

17. ***Orns****- Ornaments.*

18. ***Chaturangini Army****- Name of Pandavas army which includes Horses, Elephants, Chariots, and soldiers on foot.*

19. ***Brat****- brother.*

20. ***Bro****- brother.*

21. ***Wingy creature****- Bird.*

22. ***Black bird****- Crow.*

23. ***Black long creeper****- serpent.*

24. ***Its gem****- Serpent's gem (Naag Mani) In Indian folk stories some Serpents have an enchanted gem (Mani) which is very dear to them even more than their life*

25. ***Lord of religion****- Yudhishthira, the eldest brother in Pandavas is assumed to be the incarnation of lord of religion.*

26. ***Black God's time****- The golden time when the great lord Krishna lived. Lord Krishna face color is assumed to be black.*

27. ***Orns****- ornaments.*

28. ***Uncosted****- The cost of which can't be calculated in the gambling hall.*

29. ***Pratikami****- The name of the doorman.*

30. ***Then a camel's........vastest mounts****- it's a famous Indian Proverb – A camel is always proud of its height but when it reaches under a huge mountain, its pride breaks.*

31. ***Dushashana****-The younger brother of Duryodhana.*

*32.**Dis-action**- Bad activity.*

*33. **CHEERHARANA**- the shameful act of trying a lady make strip.*

*34.**Kshatriyas**- the caste of kings.*

*35.**Kshatritwa**- Proud of being a Kshatriya.*

*36. **She**- here she means a lady.*

*37.**Single beat**- only one curse.*

*38. **Bings**- (Pile) but here virtues.*

9 798885 036559

Printed by Libri Plureos GmbH in Hamburg,
Germany